Original title:
New Love, New Me

Copyright © 2024 Swan Charm
All rights reserved.

Author: Kene Elistrand
ISBN HARDBACK: 978-9916-89-936-6
ISBN PAPERBACK: 978-9916-89-937-3
ISBN EBOOK: 978-9916-89-938-0

Soul's Rebirth in Radiance

In shadows cast, a whisper calls,
Awakening spirit, breaking walls.
From ashes rise, the heart anew,
In love's embrace, the soul breaks through.

Each tear a seed, in faith we sow,
A garden blooms where grace will flow.
The light will guide, through night so deep,
In holy rest, our spirits leap.

From darkness formed, a luminous dawn,
In sacred light, our fears are gone.
Transcend the pain, and seek the whole,
In radiant arms, we heal the soul.

In the Light of Affection

Beneath the stars, love's gentle glow,
In tender hearts, our spirits grow.
With every breath, a prayer we weave,
In bonds of trust, we shall believe.

Soft whispers shared, in silence sweet,
Divine connections, where souls meet.
Through trials faced, we stand as one,
In light of affection, the battle's won.

As rays of hope, through darkness flow,
In love's reflection, we come to know.
The warmth of grace, eternally flows,
In the light of affection, our faith glows.

Transcendent Joys

In valleys low, where sorrow dwells,
A song of joy, our spirit tells.
Through grace bestowed, we lift our eyes,
To dance with stars in endless skies.

Each heartbeat sings, a melody,
The gift of life, our symphony.
In gratitude, we find our way,
Transcendent joys in every day.

With open hearts, we share our light,
In unity, we banish night.
A world reborn, in love's pure glow,
Transcendent joys, together flow.

The Path to Salvation

On winding roads where faith resides,
We walk together, as love guides.
With every step, our burdens shed,
Towards sacred truth, our spirits led.

Through trials faced, in faith we stand,
United hearts, a trusted band.
With open eyes, we seek the light,
In shadows deep, we find our sight.

The path is steep, yet filled with grace,
In every struggle, a sacred place.
With love as our guide, we shall prevail,
On the path to salvation, we never fail.

Seraphim's Dance of Discovery

In the realm where angels soar,
Wisdom shines forevermore.
With wings that spread like whispers sweet,
They guide our souls on sacred beat.

Through the veil of time they glide,
In ethereal grace, they abide.
A dance of light, a heavenly song,
In unity, where all belong.

Each step unveils the Divine plan,
In gentle rhythms, hand in hand.
Beneath the stars, in purest glow,
Seraphim bring what we seek to know.

Awakening hearts with every twirl,
Transforming pain into a pearl.
Through sacred movements, spirits rise,
Touching the depth of cosmic skies.

A melody of hope, a sigh of grace,
We find our path in this warm embrace.
In each soft leap, we discover more,
Seraphim lead to the open door.

Transcendence in Tenderness

In the stillness of the night,
Whispers of love take flight.
Gentle touch, a soothing balm,
Carries the spirit to a calm.

In the heart where kindness blooms,
Hope dispels the darkest glooms.
Each act of grace, a bridge to God,
Upon this path, we shall not trod.

Embraced in arms of endless care,
Transcendence found in sacred prayer.
A quiet strength, divinely poured,
In tenderness, we find the Lord.

With every moment shared and spent,
Life's bitter turns become content.
For in the warmth of hearts that beat,
Transcendence flows, and spirits greet.

The Light Beyond First Glance

Beneath the veil of worldly sight,
There lies a truth, so pure, so bright.
When shadows whisper and clouds obscure,
The heart's keen eye shall see for sure.

A glimmer shines from deep within,
Illuminating where love's been.
Each moment holds a spark of grace,
To guide the lost to a sacred place.

Beyond the surface, life reveals,
A tapestry that softly heals.
In silence, wisdom takes its stand,
The light of God is close at hand.

We seek not just the fleeting glow,
But depths where sacred rivers flow.
In every heart, the divine trace,
The light that shimmers, our saving grace.

Renewal Through Celestial Connection

When the stars weave tales above,
They speak of hope, they sing of love.
In the silence of a prayer,
We find the peace that lingers there.

In cosmic arms, our spirits rise,
As we open wide to the skies.
A union forged in heavenly fire,
Ignites the heart with pure desire.

Renewal flows from this embrace,
Awakening truth in hidden space.
Each heartbeat echoes the Creator's song,
In celestial connection, we all belong.

The universe whispers, softly clear,
In every heartbeat, love draws near.
A sacred bond, eternally sealed,
Through cosmic grace, our fate revealed.

Love's Holy Retreat

In silence deep, the heart does weep,
Where faith and love in shadows creep.
The soul finds peace in whispered prayer,
In sacred space, we breathe the air.

With open hands, we give our trust,
In love's embrace, we find what's just.
Each gentle word a soft caress,
Transforming pain into blessed rest.

Beneath the stars, our spirits soar,
United here, forevermore.
In every heartbeat, divine grace shines,
A love eternal, sacred lines.

Together we walk this hallowed ground,
In each step, echoes of hope abound.
With every smile, a spark ignites,
In love's retreat, we find our light.

So let us dwell in holy peace,
Where fears dissolve and tensions cease.
In love's retreat, our souls align,
An endless bond, a love divine.

Tranquility in Touch

In gentle touch, our spirits blend,
A sacred bond that will not end.
Through every glance, a silent prayer,
In tranquil moments, love lays bare.

With every breath, we share the grace,
In soft embrace, we find our place.
The warmth of you, a guiding light,
In darkness deep, you shine so bright.

Let fingers weave a tender thread,
In unity where dreams are fed.
With every heartbeat, love's song flows,
In tranquil touch, all fear quickly goes.

In moments still, our hearts collide,
Together in faith, we brave the tide.
With open souls, in love we trust,
In tranquil touch, we rise from dust.

So come, my love, let silence speak,
In every heartbeat, hear the weak.
A tranquil world, just you and I,
In love's embrace, we'll soar and fly.

The Blessing of You

In every glance, the heavens sing,
A blessing born on angel's wing.
With tender grace, you light the way,
A guiding star through night and day.

Your laughter dances like the breeze,
A whispered prayer that brings me ease.
In every tear, a story told,
Of love enduring, brave and bold.

With every smile, a sacred spark,
You chase away the deepening dark.
Together, hand in hand we stand,
In love's embrace, forever planned.

Through trials faced, our faith holds strong,
In your sweet arms, I know I belong.
The blessing of you, my heart's delight,
A beacon shining through the night.

So let us dance in joy divine,
With every step, your heart entwined.
In gratitude for all we do,
I find my peace in the blessing of you.

Reflections of Divine Affection

In quiet moments, love reveals,
A gentle truth that softly heals.
Through every glance, a spark ignites,
Reflections deep on starry nights.

The heart unfolds like petals fair,
In tender love, we find our prayer.
With every breath, the spirit glows,
A dance of souls where compassion flows.

In every trial, we find our strength,
In love's embrace, we go the length.
The divine whispers within our core,
In gracious echoes, we seek for more.

With every sunset, blessings shine,
In sacred stillness, your hand in mine.
Reflections of love, pure and true,
In every moment, I see the you.

So let us walk this path of grace,
With open hearts, a warm embrace.
In love's reflection, we see the light,
A divine connection, forever bright.

Elysian Fields of Affection

In the garden of grace we walk,
Hand in hand, our hearts unlock.
Under sunlit skies we find,
Love entwined, two souls aligned.

In the whispers of the breeze,
Promise blooms among the trees.
With every step, we share the light,
Guided by the stars so bright.

In the valley where dreams reside,
Faith and hope stand side by side.
With gentle hands, we lift our prayer,
In these fields, we find our care.

Through the trials, love remains,
In the storm, it calms the pains.
Each moment shared, a sacred song,
In this bond, we belong.

Elysian warmth, forever found,
In affection's holy ground.
Together we shall always tread,
In this love, our spirits fed.

The Faith of Finding Each Other

In the silence of a prayer,
We seek the love that lingers there.
Hearts entwined by fate's design,
In the tapestry, your heart is mine.

Through the trials that life bestows,
In each shadow, our light grows.
Faithful steps, hand in hand,
In love's embrace, we firmly stand.

In a world of fleeting time,
We dance to destiny's rhyme.
With every glance, a spark ignites,
Leading us through darkest nights.

In the echo of our laughter,
Hope resides, now and after.
With every word, we build the way,
Guided by love, come what may.

The faith we have will never fade,
In our hearts, a serenade.
Together we rise, forever bold,
In the warmth of love we hold.

Illuminated Souls on Sacred Ground

In the glow of sacred light,
Two souls merge, a wondrous sight.
Guided by a higher call,
In love's embrace, we rise, we fall.

With each heartbeat, we proclaim,
In the stillness, we find our name.
Dancing in the twilight's grace,
In this moment, we embrace.

The universe aligns our fates,
As destiny patiently waits.
A bond unbreakable, pure, and bright,
In the sacred silence of the night.

Every challenge that we face,
Carved in love, no time can erase.
On this hallowed ground we stand,
With open hearts, we hold His hand.

Illuminated by the stars,
Together, healing all our scars.
In the rhythm of the divine,
In love, forever we entwine.

Serendipity's Covenant in the Stars

By chance, our paths, like fate in flight,
Brought us forth to this sacred light.
In the cosmic dance, we find our way,
A covenant that none can sway.

In the whispers of the night sky,
We weave our dreams, you and I.
With every spark, our souls ignite,
Bound together, hearts alight.

With stars as witnesses above,
We write the stories of our love.
In serendipity's sweet embrace,
Together we carve out our place.

Guided by the moon's soft glow,
In eternal ebb and flow.
Our hearts align with every beat,
In this harmony, we are complete.

A celestial bond, bright and true,
In this life, I choose you.
Ours is a tale, written in time,
Serendipity's love, forever sublime.

Spiritual Connection

In silence, we seek the divine,
Hearts whisper, souls entwine.
Through shadows, light shall guide,
In faith, we will abide.

The path is steep, yet pure,
With love, our hearts endure.
In prayer, we find our grace,
Together in this sacred space.

Each moment, a breath of peace,
In this bond, our worries cease.
We rise as one, in holy song,
With trust, we all belong.

Through trials, our spirits soar,
In unity, we implore.
With hope, we lift our gaze,
In gratitude, we sing His praise.

Together we wander, hand in hand,
In faith, we firmly stand.
With love, the world we share,
In every heart, He's there.

Adoration's Journey

With every step, we seek the light,
In shadows deep, we find our sight.
Through valleys low and mountains high,
In adoration, our spirits fly.

To worship with each beat of heart,
In every soul, we play our part.
With humble thanks, we lift our voice,
In faith, we make our choice.

The road is long, yet filled with grace,
In trials, we find His face.
With trust, we walk this sacred way,
In love, our fears decay.

In silence, we hear His call,
Together we rise, never to fall.
With pure devotion, we stand still,
In His embrace, we find our will.

The journey's end, a promise bright,
In His arms, we find our light.
With gratitude, we shine and share,
In adoration, nothing can compare.

The Fellowship of Hearts

In love and faith, we gather near,
To lift each other, shed a tear.
With open hearts, we share our pain,
In this fellowship, we gain.

Through laughter and through strife,
We honor each precious life.
In unity, we walk this road,
With kindness, we lighten the load.

In prayers shared, we find our peace,
In every hug, our worries cease.
With gentle words, we help to mend,
In our hearts, we find a friend.

Together, we rise with every fall,
In hope and love, we heed the call.
With open arms, we reach for grace,
In this fellowship, we find our place.

In moments bright, in shadows cast,
With faith and love, we hold steadfast.
With joy, our spirits intertwine,
In fellowship, His light will shine.

A Testament of Transitions

In every change, a lesson lies,
With every tear, our spirit flies.
Through seasons of both joy and strife,
In transitions, we find life.

With faith, we embrace the unknown,
In trials faced, our strength is shown.
In moments grave, we learn to trust,
In transformation, we find what's just.

The winding road may seem unclear,
Yet in His love, we hold no fear.
With every step, a new path grows,
In faith and hope, our spirit flows.

Through night and day, we forge ahead,
In every chapter, the spirit's fed.
With gratitude, we meet each dawn,
In transitions, we are reborn.

Though change is often hard to bear,
In His light, we find our care.
With lessons learned, we stand anew,
In transitions, His love is true.

Heaven's Embrace

In the light where angels sing,
Heaven's joy begins to ring.
Softly in the dawn's warm glow,
Peace descends, with love bestowed.

Golden rays on tender skin,
Washing all the doubt within.
In this place where spirits soar,
Heaven's embrace forevermore.

Guiding us through trials deep,
Promises that we shall keep.
Through the storms, our faith will lead,
In His love, we are freed.

Life's journey bears a sacred plan,
Hand in hand, we understand.
Each step blessed by grace divine,
Heaven's truth is mine and thine.

As we walk on paths so bright,
Hearts ignite with purest light.
In the stillness, hear the plea,
Come and dwell in harmony.

The Renewal of the Heart

With every dawn, the heart revives,
In the stillness, the spirit thrives.
Cleansing tears fall like the rain,
Washing away all past pain.

A tender touch, a whispered prayer,
Renewal found in love's warm glare.
Grace flows softly, pure and true,
Heart reborn, with each day new.

In the silence of the night,
Faith ignites a hopeful light.
With each struggle, strength we gain,
In the darkness, love remains.

Hear the call of the divine,
In the chaos, let us find,
Every heartbeat sings the song,
In His embrace, we belong.

Through valleys deep, and mountains high,
Our spirits soar, we learn to fly.
Trust the journey, never part,
Awake, arise, renew the heart.

Awakening in Grace

Beneath the stars, where shadows play,
Awakening leads us the way.
In stillness, hear the quiet word,
Within the heart, his voice is heard.

Moments rise like morning dew,
Glistening hope in all we do.
Each breath a sacred hymn of praise,
Awakening in gentle grace.

The world unfolds in vibrant hue,
Illuminated by love so true.
With open hearts and open minds,
In sacred unity, peace we find.

As nature sings her sweet refrain,
We learn to dance through joy and pain.
Every step a chance to see,
Awakening brings us to be free.

In the quiet of the night,
Stars bear witness to our plight.
Awakened to the love that waits,
Grace descends and liberates.

Divine Whispers in the Night

In the twilight, shadows creep,
A quiet call that stirs from sleep.
Divine whispers float on air,
Softly guiding through despair.

Stars above, a shimmering light,
Telling tales of love's delight.
In the silence, faith takes flight,
Hearts entwined in sacred sight.

Winds of change begin to blow,
Offering peace where sorrows flow.
In the depths of night we seek,
The gentle words, the love we speak.

Every moment, grace bestowed,
Pathways bright where angels trod.
In surrender, we find our way,
Through divine whispers, night to day.

Trust in love, it will abide,
In the shadows, you'll confide.
Divine whispers lead us home,
Through the night, we're never alone.

Blessed Moments

In quietude, I seek Your grace,
Each breath a prayer, a sacred space.
The sun that rises, the stars that gleam,
Whisper of love, a holy dream.

In laughter shared, in tears that flow,
A touch of warmth, Your love to show.
In fleeting time, in still of night,
Your presence lingers, pure delight.

With every heartbeat, I feel Your light,
Guiding my path, dispelling fright.
In each embrace, a gift I find,
A glimpse of You, in heart and mind.

Through trials faced, I stand in trust,
In faith I grow, not in the dust.
Your blessings rain, like sweet perfume,
Transforming shadows, making bloom.

In sacred moments, I dwell in peace,
My spirit lifts, my worries cease.
Forever held in love's sweet hand,
With blessed moments, I truly stand.

Cherished Offerings

With open hands, I give my heart,
To You, my Lord, a sacred start.
In offering love, I draw so near,
In humble service, I cast my fear.

Each prayer I send, a fragrant gift,
In gratitude, my spirits lift.
The quiet moments, I share with glee,
Become cherished offerings, pure and free.

In daily acts, I find Your grace,
In every smile, I see Your face.
In kindness shown, a holy deed,
Through every heart, Your love we heed.

The songs I sing, in worship bright,
Illuminate the darkest night.
In every note, I weave a prayer,
To lift the world, to show I care.

Cherished offerings, a bounteous feast,
In giving love, I am released.
With every breath, I seek to serve,
In Your embrace, I find resolve.

Soul-Stirring Devotion

Oh, soul-stirring love that never fades,
In every moment, Your light cascades.
With fervent heart, I turn to You,
In every struggle, my faith rings true.

From mountain peaks to valleys low,
In every breath, Your goodness flows.
I set my gaze on heaven's throne,
In silent moments, I'm never alone.

Each tender whisper, a guiding star,
Leads me closer, no matter how far.
In fervor deep, I seek to know,
The depths of love that ever grow.

Your sacred word, my heart's delight,
A beacon shining through the night.
In every trial, I cling to grace,
In soul-stirring devotion, I find my place.

Oh, let me walk this path of light,
With You beside me, all fears take flight.
In hands of love, my soul will soar,
In every heartbeat, I long for more.

Hallowed Heartstrings

In hallowed halls where echoes rise,
I find Your presence, beyond the skies.
Each heartbeat dances, strings entwined,
In sacred melody, our souls aligned.

With every prayer, a note of grace,
In worship whispered, I seek Your face.
The music flows, a gentle stream,
Hallowed heartstrings weave a dream.

In trials faced, I sing aloud,
A hymn of faith, proud and unbowed.
Within Your arms, the sorrows cease,
In every lyric, I find my peace.

Through night and day, Your love holds tight,
Illuminating darkness with pure light.
In harmony, our spirits sing,
In hallowed heartstrings, hope does cling.

With grateful heart, I live each day,
In service true, I find my way.
Forever bound by love's embrace,
In hallowed heartstrings, I find my place.

Hymn of the Unseen Bond

In shadows deep, we find our way,
A thread of light to guide the stray.
Through trials fierce, we join our hands,
In faith, we stand, our spirit's strands.

Each whispered prayer, a sacred song,
In unity, we grow more strong.
The unseen bond, it holds us tight,
In darkest hours, we'll seek the light.

With every heartbeat, trust does rise,
In love's embrace, we touch the skies.
For in this journey, side by side,
The soul's own truth shall be our guide.

Through storms and strife, we shall endure,
In sacred vows, our hearts are pure.
Together, we will pave the way,
With every dawn, a new bouquet.

As holy whispers fill the air,
We'll weave our hopes, a tapestry rare.
In gratitude, we lift our voice,
For in each other, we rejoice.

Redemption in the Embrace of Another

In silent chambers, grace is born,
From broken paths, new dreams are worn.
With open hearts, we gather near,
In love's embrace, we hold no fear.

Through burdens shared, our spirits rise,
Each tear we shed, a sweet surprise.
For in your arms, I find my peace,
A warm cocoon, where sorrows cease.

The mirror holds our souls entwined,
In every glance, a truth defined.
With gentle hands, we heal our scars,
We're bound together, like the stars.

In whispered prayers, our hopes ignite,
Two flames converge, a single light.
From ashes born, our love will bloom,
In faith's embrace, we banish gloom.

As seasons change, our roots grow strong,
In this sweet dance, we both belong.
With every heartbeat, grace will find,
Redemption shines, two souls aligned.

The Prayer of Hearts Entwined

O gentle spirit, hear my plea,
In every heartbeat, let us be.
With hands united, hearts exposed,
In sacred trust, our love is closed.

In trials faced, let us not sway,
For in your light, I find my way.
With every step, a prayer we share,
In moments cherished, we find our care.

As stars align, our path will shine,
In faith we walk, your hand in mine.
With whispered thoughts, the heavens call,
Together we shall rise, not fall.

In laughter shared and joy profound,
A melody in love is found.
In quiet hours, our spirits blend,
In endless grace, on you depend.

Our journey long, yet beautifully clear,
In every heartbeat, I draw you near.
With every prayer, our souls ignite,
A tapestry of endless light.

Celestial Blossoms in a Shared Garden

In sacred soil, our roots entwine,
With gentle hands, your heart is mine.
Each bloom we seek, in love's own grace,
A garden grows, a holy place.

With tender care, we water dreams,
In moonlit nights, hear soft heart beams.
For every petal kissed by dew,
Reflects the love that springs anew.

The fragrance sweet, it lifts our souls,
In harmony, our spirits whole.
Together we sing, a joyful tune,
Beneath the watchful sun and moon.

As seasons change, we shall uphold,
The promise made, the story told.
Through trials faced and laughter shared,
In every truth, our hearts declared.

In this divine, enchanted plot,
With every bloom, we're dearly sought.
In love's embrace, forever stay,
Celestial blossoms light the way.

Spirit's Embrace

In the quiet of the dawn, we find,
Whispers of the spirit, gentle and kind.
A touch of love, a guiding light,
In shadows deep, we seek the bright.

The heart awakes, a sacred bell,
In every breath, a story to tell.
With every step, we feel the grace,
Embraced by love in this holy space.

Upon the altar, our hopes ignite,
Dreams woven in the fabric of night.
In sacred rhythms, our souls entwine,
Together in faith, forever we shine.

Through trials faced, we rise anew,
Strengthened by love, pure and true.
In moments frail, we find our way,
In spirit's embrace, we choose to stay.

United as one, we journey far,
Guided by love, our radiant star.
In every heartbeat, the spirit draws near,
In sacred whispers, we know no fear.

A Testament of Affection

Within our hearts the echoes sing,
Of love divine, its gentle wing.
Each moment shared, a sacred vow,
A testament of affection now.

In each embrace, the world stands still,
Bound by the warmth of love's sweet thrill.
Through trials faced and darkness fought,
A bond unbroken, with faith we sought.

Let kindness be the language learned,
In every touch, a lantern burned.
For in our hearts, the truth remains,
A testament in love's refrains.

With open arms, we welcome grace,
In every smile, we seek His face.
Together we walk, hand in hand,
A testament of love, forever we stand.

As seasons change and shadows fall,
His guiding light will hear our call.
With hearts ablaze and spirits wide,
A testament of love, our sacred guide.

Awakening of the Heart

In stillness found, the heart awakes,
A gentle whisper, the spirit breaks.
With every dawn, a brand new start,
The sacred space of the opened heart.

Through trials faced, the spirit soars,
In shadows cast, it bravely roars.
With every heartbeat, love's refrain,
An awakening, breaking the chains.

In radiant hues, the world appears,
A dance of joy, dissolving fears.
Through storms we sail, with faith as our art,
Together we rise, awakening heart.

Within the silence, a voice resounds,
In sacred echoes, hope abounds.
With every step on this hallowed ground,
An awakening of love profound.

In unity we find the key,
To open hearts that long to be free.
Embraced in grace, we take our part,
In the sacred journey, awakening heart.

Divine Embrace of Change

In every season, the winds will change,
A dance of life, both wild and strange.
With open hearts, we greet the new,
In divine embrace, our spirits grew.

Through every twist, uncertainty reigns,
Yet in its arms, a grace remains.
With courage found, we shift the tide,
In divine embrace, we choose to bide.

The river flows, a testament bright,
Of strength to change, our guiding light.
In harmony found, we learn to bend,
In the divine embrace, our hearts will mend.

Each moment a gift, a lesson learned,
In twilight's glow, our souls discerned.
With faith in hand, we walk the way,
Embraced by change, we find our stay.

For in the ebb, there's grace to see,
A divine embrace, we choose to be free.
With every heartbeat, we sign our name,
In love's vast ocean, we play the game.

A Covenant of Hearts

In silent prayer we gather here,
A promise held, so pure and clear.
Hearts entwined in sacred pact,
In love's embrace, we won't look back.

Through trials faced and shadows cast,
Our faith will bridge the void so vast.
With every tear, a strength we find,
In unity, our souls aligned.

We journey forth, two paths as one,
Through storms and suns, we are not done.
The covenant holds, it won't break,
In every choice, our hearts awake.

With gentle words, we build our way,
In kindness, pure, come what may.
Together we stand, in joy, in strife,
A sacred bond, our shared life.

So let this pact forever stand,
Together strong, hand in hand.
In faith and love, we find our start,
A holy truth, a covenant of hearts.

Guided by the Spirit

In quiet stillness, we seek the light,
A guiding force, both gentle and bright.
With whispered winds and sacred sign,
The Spirit leads our hearts to shine.

Each step we take, in trust we move,
Through all the challenges, we improve.
With faith as our armor, we'll stand tall,
In the spirit's love, we'll never fall.

With open hearts, we feel the call,
To serve each other, to lift and enthrall.
In every struggle, we find our way,
With the Spirit's grace, we choose to stay.

As stars align in the night's embrace,
We gather strength, we find our place.
In harmony's song, our spirits soar,
Together bound, forevermore.

So let us walk with eyes so bright,
Guided always by the light.
In every breath, in every sigh,
With Spirit's love, we'll never die.

Trusting the Divine Design

In every heartbeat, a purpose found,
A tapestry of love unbound.
With threads of grace, each moment we weave,
Trust in the plan, together believe.

Each mountain high, each valley low,
In faith, we learn, in love we grow.
Every step is a sacred dance,
In God's embrace, we take our chance.

Through trials faced and answers sought,
In learning, wisdom is gently taught.
With every scar, a story shared,
A map of life, divinely prepared.

The beauty in chaos, the peace in pain,
In trusting the path, we break the chain.
With open hearts, we take the ride,
In the divine's hands, we confide.

So let us walk, with spirits aligned,
Embracing love, the grand design.
With faith as our compass, we will go,
Forever trusting in what we sow.

The Sanctuary of Affection

In every smile, a refuge found,
A soft embrace where love abounds.
In gentle whispers, hearts entwine,
A sanctuary, sacred and divine.

Through every storm, in quiet grace,
Affection blooms in every space.
With open arms, we gather near,
In unity's warmth, we banish fear.

With laughter shared and tears embraced,
The beauty of life is interlaced.
In moments sweet, our spirits rise,
In love's embrace, we touch the skies.

Together we build our sacred ground,
In every heartbeat, love is found.
With faith as our foundation strong,
In the sanctuary, we all belong.

So let our hearts be ever true,
In love's embrace, we'll start anew.
With every breath, in every view,
In this sanctuary, me and you.

A New Psalm for Life's Journey

In the stillness of dawn's grace,
I seek Your path, O Holy Light.
With each step, my fears embrace,
Your love guides me through the night.

Mountains rise, yet I am bold,
With faith, my spirit takes flight.
In Your hands, my dreams unfold,
Together, we shine ever bright.

Through valleys deep and rivers wide,
You are my strength, my heart's song.
With every tear, I'm purified,
In Your arms, I truly belong.

The path is steep, but I shall tread,
For You comfort my weary soul.
In moments lost, let hope be fed,
Your promises make me whole.

As life flows on, I walk with grace,
Each moment a gift divine.
In Your love, I find my place,
Forever, I am truly Thine.

Refuge of the Intertwined Hearts

In the garden where love grows,
Two hearts join in sacred trust.
Amidst the thorns, our spirit flows,
Together, we rise from dust.

Your whispers calm the raging sea,
In storms of life, our bond holds true.
As branches entwine, so will we,
In faith, surrounded by the dew.

When shadows fall and hopes seem lost,
We gather light, dispel the night.
In sacrifice, love pays the cost,
Together, we find the path so bright.

With gentleness, we tread the way,
Each heartbeat echoes heaven's song.
In service and joy, we will stay,
In unity, we shall grow strong.

Through trials, our love shall sustain,
In the refuge of each embrace.
With faith, we'll take joy from the pain,
Intertwined, we're bound in grace.

Journeys to the Throne of Togetherness

Together we venture through time's embrace,
Hand in hand, the challenges faced.
In laughter and tears, we share the space,
To the throne of grace, our hearts interlaced.

With every step, we seek Your light,
In the quiet, we find our song.
Together, we conquer the endless night,
In Your love, O Lord, we belong.

Through winding paths and open skies,
Our spirits soar, forever free.
As the dawn breaks, love never dies,
In unity, we find our glee.

In valleys low, Your blessings flow,
Our hearts join in peaceful prayer.
Together we thrive, together we grow,
In the grace of love, we're laid bare.

Across the hills, our dreams arise,
Guided by Your gentle hand.
Journeys of love beneath vast skies,
Together, we shall ever stand.

The Sacred Union of Kindred Spirits

Beneath the stars, our souls converge,
In silent vows, our spirits dance.
With every heartbeat, love does surge,
A symphony of sacred chance.

In laughter's glow and sorrow's shade,
Our bond entwines in holy grace.
With faith, through every choice we've made,
Together, we journey, face to face.

As seasons change, we too shall grow,
In harmony, we walk the land.
With gentle hands, we'll reap what we sow,
In understanding, we make our stand.

When trials rise like tempest's roar,
Our love remains a steadfast guide.
In kindred spirit, we restore,
Together still, we will abide.

So here we stand, hand in hand,
Beacons of hope, forever bright.
In sacred union, we make our stand,
Hearts united, blessed in light.

Celestial Echoes

In heaven's choir, a resounding song,
Voices lifted, where we all belong.
Stars align in a divine embrace,
Guiding us through time and space.

Wonders whispered in the night,
Promises of hope, a shining light.
Creation's breath, in silence profound,
In celestial echoes, love is found.

Each prayer sent, a gentle breeze,
Carried forth with such sweet ease.
In every heart, a sacred spark,
Rekindled faith when days grow dark.

Nature sings in harmony,
With every leaf, a symphony.
Mountains bow, rivers flow,
In the dance of life, we grow.

So heed the call, the spirit's voice,
In all creation, we rejoice.
Together we rise, hand in hand,
In celestial echoes, we will stand.

Pillars of Trust

In shadows deep, where fears reside,
We seek the strength where love abides.
Pillars rise, steadfast and true,
A sanctuary built for me and you.

Each word we share, a sacred bond,
In trials faced, the heart grows fond.
With every promise, we build a wall,
A fortress strong, we will not fall.

Through storms of doubt, together we brave,
In the arms of trust, we find our save.
Unified faith in graceful gaze,
Illuminates our winding ways.

With open hearts, we share our plight,
In darkest moments, ignite the light.
Together we rise, embracing fate,
For love is stronger, never late.

So let us stand, both firm and bold,
In this fortress, our story is told.
Pillars of trust, forever reign,
In every joy, in every pain.

The Genesis of Togetherness

From solitude, a spark ignites,
In hearts entwined, we find our rights.
Together we forge this sacred path,
In the dance of love, we witness wrath.

In the tapestry of fate, we weave,
Threads of hope, we truly believe.
In our unity, strength is found,
In every heartbeat, love unbound.

As seasons change, we hold the line,
In trials faced, our spirits shine.
With every step, we grow and learn,
In this genesis, we brightly burn.

Through laughter shared and sorrows cried,
We find our way with hearts open wide.
Together we share this earthly quest,
In togetherness, we are our best.

So let us treasure this sacred bond,
In every moment, of which we're fond.
For love's pure light, forever glows,
In the genesis of the life we chose.

Embracing Sacred Light

In whispered prayers, our spirits rise,
To realms alight, beyond the skies.
With every dawn, we seek the grace,
In embracing light, we find our place.

In shadows cast, hope's ember glows,
Revealing paths where mercy flows.
With open hearts, we learn to fly,
In sacred light, love will not die.

As nature blooms in colors bright,
We stand together, hearts alight.
In every smile, a spark ignites,
We're woven close in endless sights.

Through trials faced, we gather near,
In every battle, cast away fear.
In unity, we claim our fight,
In strength awakened by sacred light.

So let us shine, both near and far,
In every moment, just as we are.
Together we rise, hearts intertwined,
In embracing sacred light, we find.

Heartfelt Benediction

In silence we lift our hearts in prayer,
Trusting the light that guides us there.
With love encircling every soul,
We find strength in the one and whole.

May peace rest softly on our brow,
In gentle moments, here and now.
The spirit flows, a sacred stream,
Awakening us to every dream.

Together we walk this blessed land,
With faith unbroken, hand in hand.
In each other's eyes, the love we see,
Echoes the light of eternity.

Our voices rise in harmonies sweet,
In gratitude, our hearts we greet.
For every blessing that we share,
Reminds us of the love laid bare.

So let us go with humble grace,
Embracing each moment, each place.
For in this life, we truly find,
The love of the source, intertwined.

Whispers of the Divine

In the quiet, when shadows play,
I hear the whispers, guide my way.
Softly spoken, truth unfolds,
A sacred story, in hearts it holds.

Each dawning sun brings hope anew,
With every breath, I feel it too.
The gentle touch of heaven's grace,
Enfolding all in warm embrace.

Oft in stillness, the soul takes flight,
Finding solace in the light.
As rivers flow, so love will stream,
Binding the hearts in a holy dream.

Under stars that brightly gleam,
We wander forth, like a midnight beam.
In unity, we rise and sing,
To the joy that every moment brings.

Let us gather, hand in hand,
Creating peace across the land.
In every whisper, divine and pure,
Together, our spirits shall endure.

The Anointing of Togetherness

In every heart, a spark ignites,
Guiding us through the darkest nights.
With every prayer, our hopes align,
Anointing love, a holy sign.

Let kindness flow like healing rain,
Softening edges, easing pain.
In the embrace of common grace,
We find our truth in this sacred space.

As community, we rise as one,
Chasing the shadows, welcoming the sun.
The bond we hold, a treasured gift,
Lifting each other, spirits uplift.

From diverse paths, we find our way,
In laughter shared, or in words we pray.
Anointing moments, forever blessed,
In faith and love, we find our rest.

So may we walk through life divine,
With open hearts, our souls entwine.
Together blessed, for all to see,
In the anointing of unity.

Abundant Grace

In shadows deep, grace shines bright,
A beacon glowing through the night.
With open hands, we gather near,
Embracing moments, love sincere.

Each breath a gift, each heartbeat true,
In gratitude, we start anew.
With hearts aligned, we lift our song,
In harmony, we all belong.

May mercy flow like rivers wide,
With faith embraced, we shall abide.
For in this journey, hand in hand,
We weave the fabric of this land.

Let us remember, as we strive,
That kindness sets our souls alive.
In every challenge, grace we find,
A love unbounded, intertwined.

So as we walk in faith's embrace,
May joy be ours, in every place.
With hearts aglow, we share the space,
Together living, in abundant grace.

Faith's Tender Blossom

In gardens where the lilies grow,
A whisper of the heart's soft glow.
Each petal drenched in morning dew,
A promise old, a vision true.

In trials fierce, we seek the light,
A guiding star, our beacon bright.
With roots that stretch through pain and strife,
We nurture hope, embrace our life.

Through storms that rage and shadows cast,
The faith we hold will ever last.
Like blooms that turn to face the sun,
Together, we will overcome.

In quiet prayers and sacred songs,
Our spirit dances, where it belongs.
In every heart, a seed is sown,
A tender blossom, love has grown.

Reverence in Every Touch

In every glance, a sacred grace,
A glimpse of You in this dear place.
With gentle hands, we break the bread,
In unity, our spirit's fed.

The hugs that bind, the smiles we share,
A connection deep, beyond compare.
In every touch, a loving spark,
Illuminating paths through dark.

With gratitude we lift our days,
As through the world, our kindness plays.
In reverence we find our way,
To honor life in all we say.

Through every trial, each tender mile,
Our faith endures, it makes us smile.
In every heart, affection grows,
With every touch, Your essence flows.

A Prayer for Togetherness

In whispering winds, our hearts unite,
A chorus sang in the still of night.
With every word, our spirits blend,
In love's embrace, our souls ascend.

A prayer for peace, on earth we send,
Each moment cherished, time to spend.
As sunbeams dance on morning's dew,
Together, Lord, we walk with You.

Through trials faced, hand in hand,
We build a bridge, we take a stand.
With open hearts, our spirits soar,
In togetherness, we seek for more.

In laughter shared, our joy rings clear,
With gratitude, we draw You near.
A prayer we weave, like stars above,
In unity, we find Your love.

The Beatitude of Us

In gentle words, we find our grace,
The beatitude of every face.
With open hands and spirits free,
We cherish life's sweet harmony.

Through valleys deep and mountains high,
Our hearts together abide, we fly.
In every laugh, a joy divine,
A sacred bond, forever shine.

The grace bestowed where kindness reigns,
In every life, love breaks the chains.
With grateful hearts, we feel the truth,
In every age, in every youth.

Through trials faced with courage bold,
Our stories weave a tapestry told.
In unity, our spirits trust,
Together bright, the beatitude of us.

A Sacred Transformation

In the silence of the night, we pray,
Awakening the souls in disarray.
With whispers of grace that bless the dawn,
We rise anew, from shadows withdrawn.

The heart, a vessel of divine light,
Guides us through the long, arduous night.
With every tear that falls to the earth,
Seeds of wisdom find their rebirth.

In the embrace of love's warm hand,
We find our place in this sacred land.
Transformation flows like a gentle stream,
Each moment crafted, a holy dream.

So let the spirits dance and sing,
For in our hearts, they take to wing.
With faith as our beacon, we stride forth,
To spread the light, to honor worth.

Together, we walk this sacred path,
In unity, we shun the aftermath.
With open hearts and minds in tune,
We celebrate the rising of the moon.

Blossoms of the Spirit

From the roots of hope, we bloom,
Emerging bright from the quiet gloom.
Each petal whispers truths untold,
A tapestry of love we behold.

In the garden where the saints reside,
Faith and grace do gently bide.
The fragrance of peace fills the air,
As hearts awaken to sacred prayer.

Sunlight beams on every face,
Illuminating each divine space.
Together, we gather, hand in hand,
To nurture life across the land.

With every breath, we spread the cheer,
In the presence of the heavenly near.
Blossoms of the spirit, radiant and free,
A symphony of souls in harmony.

So let our hearts in kindness grow,
Sharing love's light, a vibrant flow.
In the unity of truth and love's persist,
We tend the garden, we shall not resist.

Chosen by the Heart

In quiet corners of the soul,
Whispers of the heart take their toll.
Destinies woven by hands unseen,
In the tapestry of life, we glean.

Through trials faced and shadows cast,
The journey molds us, shapes us fast.
With every choice, we forge our way,
Grounded in faith, come what may.

Chosen by the heart, we rise anew,
To walk in paths where love shines through.
Each moment rich, a sacred gift,
A chance to heal, a spirit uplift.

In fellowship, we gather strong,
Singing the ancient, familiar song.
Together bound by threads of grace,
We find our home in every place.

So let us honor all we share,
With open hearts, through every prayer.
In love's embrace, we find our part,
Forever guided, chosen by the heart.

Seraphic Revelations

In the stillness of the twilight hour,
Angelic voices sing, a sacred power.
Revelations dance in the soft night air,
Caressing souls with a gentle prayer.

Heaven's light breaks through the veil,
Guiding seekers on the ancient trail.
Each truth revealed, a crystal clear,
Revealing what we hold most dear.

With wings of love, the seraphs soar,
Bringing messages from the realm of yore.
In their presence, we find peace and grace,
In their whispers, a warm embrace.

Our hearts unlock, like fragrant blooms,
In the light, there are no more glooms.
Together in spirit, we rise above,
United in the beauty of divine love.

So let us gather, sing and pray,
In the light of truth, with every sway.
Through seraphic revelations, our spirits ignite,
In the glow of faith, we find our light.

Heralds of Hope in the Night

In shadows deep, a light will gleam,
A guiding star, our silent dream,
With whispers soft, the dawn will rise,
Heralding hope beyond the skies.

In quiet prayers, our voices meet,
With every heartbeat, love's refrain sweet,
Together we stand, though darkness near,
Faith ignites warmth to quell our fear.

The night shall fade, the day will shine,
In unity, our spirits entwine,
With grace we walk this sacred path,
Embracing joy, dismissing wrath.

Each step we take, in peace we find,
In every heart, divine love's kind,
Together we sing, our souls ignite,
Heralds of hope in the quiet night.

Testament of Heartfelt Whispers

In gentle tones, our spirits soar,
With heartfelt whispers, we implore,
Each breath a prayer, a bond unseen,
In sharing love, we become keen.

Through trials faced, our voices blend,
In sacred trust, we learn to mend,
With every tear, a joy reborn,
In unity, the light of dawn.

The echoes linger, truth shall thrive,
In moments shared, we feel alive,
With every heartbeat, bonds entwine,
A testament of love divine.

With open hearts, we walk this way,
In whispered faith, we choose to stay,
Together strong, a sacred vow,
In heartfelt whispers, we find how.

Ascendancy of Connected Souls

In unity, our spirits rise,
Connected souls beneath the skies,
With every pulse, a rhythm shared,
In love's embrace, we are declared.

Through trials faced, we gather strength,
In bonds of grace, we find our length,
As one we soar, a sacred flight,
Ascendancy in the soft night light.

Each story shared, a thread we weave,
In every heart, we learn to believe,
Together strong, we light the way,
In love's ascent, we choose to stay.

Wherever we go, our spirits dance,
In harmony's song, we find our chance,
With every step, our essence whole,
Ascendancy of connected souls.

The Language of Celestial Affection

In every glance, a love profound,
The whispers of the stars resound,
In silent peace, our hearts converse,
The language of love, a sacred verse.

Through cosmic waves, our spirits blend,
In every touch, a message send,
In gentle caress, soft earth and sky,
Celestial affection draws us nigh.

In twilight's glow, our souls unite,
With radiant beams, dispelling night,
In harmony, we find our song,
The celestial language, where we belong.

In every heartbeat, love's refrain,
In joy and sorrow, peace we gain,
Together we rise, as stars above,
In celestial affection, we find love.

Revelations of the Heart's Awakening

In silence profound, whispers arise,
The heart's soft tune reflects the skies.
Awakening spirits in dawn's tender light,
Guiding lost souls through the deepening night.

Each beat a promise, a sacred call,
In the depths of sorrow, love conquers all.
Embrace the light, let shadows fall,
For hope is reborn, the heart stands tall.

With every tear, a story is spun,
From ashes of pain, the healing has begun.
In unity shared, the burdens we bear,
Illuminate paths, revealing our care.

Reflections of faith in each gentle sigh,
Carried on wings, where true spirits fly.
In the realm of grace, our souls intertwine,
Revealing the truth, divinely designed.

With open hands, we gather our dreams,
Bound by the love that eternally beams.
In this sacred dance, our hearts align,
Awakening visions, forever divine.

Portrait of Love's Sacred Tapestry

Threads of devotion weave through the years,
A canvas of joy, painted with tears.
Each color vibrant, each stroke sincere,
In the portrait of love, the heart draws near.

Embroidered with faith, the stories unfold,
In the warmth of embrace, the truth is told.
With laughter and grace, each moment we share,
A testament forged in the depths of care.

Golden sunbeams kiss the fabric's fold,
The warmth of our love, more precious than gold.
In twilight's embrace, our souls shall unite,
Creating a masterpiece bathed in pure light.

Each thread a reminder of journeys we've made,
In the fabric of time, true bonds never fade.
With hearts intertwined, we cherish and serve,
In this sacred tapestry, our spirits preserve.

May love be the needle that sews in the seams,
Binding our hearts like the sweetest of dreams.
In every adornment, our legacy's crest,
In the portrait of love, our souls find their rest.

Chronicles of a Heart Reborn

In shadows once cast, a light starts to bloom,
From the ashes of doubt, love's whispers consume.
The heart makes its journey through trials of pain,
Emerging with grace, like the sun after rain.

Wounds become wisdom, the scars softly blend,
In the dance of revival, the soul starts to mend.
With each tender beat, forgiveness is sown,
A garden of hope where love has been grown.

Through valleys of sorrow, through mountains of strife,
The heart learns to flourish, igniting new life.
In the embrace of the Spirit, our fears drift away,
Awakening promises woven in clay.

In stillness we gather, the stories we share,
In the song of the universe, love fills the air.
A journey of grace, from darkness to light,
Chronicles written in the stars, burning bright.

With every new dawn, a chapter unfolds,
In the book of love, the most precious of scrolls.
Through the heart's rebirth, we realize our part,
In the ever-flowing stream of a pure, sacred heart.

The Offering of Shared Dreams

In twilight's soft glow, two souls intertwine,
Dreams whisper gently, a promise divine.
With every heartbeat, intentions take flight,
In the offering shared, love glimmers bright.

With open horizons, each vision takes hold,
Together we journey, our stories unfold.
Through laughter and tears, we weave a sweet thread,
In the tapestry of life, where angels have tread.

What magic is found in the depths of the night,
When hopes are ignited and futures are bright?
In the chorus of hearts, a symphony plays,
Uniting our spirits in love's endless gaze.

As petals of spring bloom in time's gentle grace,
In the offering made, we find our true place.
Empowered by dreams that together we dream,
In the sanctuary built on love's sacred beam.

With arms wide open, we share what we hold,
The truths of our journeys, through stories retold.
In the quiet of night, as stars cast their gleam,
We honor the magic of shared, sacred dreams.

Epiphany in the Depths of Desire

In silence deep, the heart does cry,
A yearning flame that will not die.
Whispers of truth in shadows play,
Guiding the soul through night to day.

A spark ignites, a holy flame,
Awakening love, calling my name.
In depths profound, I see the light,
Desire born of divine insight.

Each breath a prayer, each sigh a song,
In tender hope, where I belong.
The sacred dance of grace unfolds,
In every heartbeat, love beholds.

A vision pure, a promise made,
By spirit's hand, my fears allayed.
In the embrace of truth sublime,
Divine connection transcends time.

Thus in the depths, my heart shall soar,
With each epiphany, I seek more.
Awash in joy, my soul's desire,
In holy light, I find my fire.

Holy Echoes of Uncharted Feelings

In stillness, echoes softly ring,
Resonant whispers of love's offering.
Through uncharted paths, I wander free,
With holy echoes beckoning me.

Each moment a gift, a sacred breath,
Awakening dreams that conquer death.
With open heart, I seek to find,
The light of grace in love entwined.

In shadows cast by doubt and fear,
The echoes call, their truth is clear.
A symphony of souls unite,
In harmony beneath the light.

With every sound, a prayer takes flight,
Transcending boundaries, pure delight.
In holy space, my heart will sing,
The song of love, eternal Spring.

Through uncharted feelings, I will tread,
Embracing all, where angels led.
In sacred whispers, I know the way,
To love's embrace, come what may.

Sanctuary Found in Another's Eyes

In gentle gaze, a refuge still,
A sanctuary where hearts will fill.
In another's eyes, I find my home,
A sacred place where spirits roam.

In silence shared, our souls collide,
With every glance, love's truth resides.
In depth of trust, we softly weave,
Together forged, we dare believe.

Through storms of life, hand in hand,
In each other's eyes, we understand.
Mirrored hearts reflecting grace,
A haven found, a warm embrace.

In tender moments, fears release,
In love's pure light, we find our peace.
Eyes deep as oceans, vast and wide,
In their embrace, I safely bide.

A sacred bond, forever strong,
In this pure sight, we both belong.
With every glance, our spirits rise,
In sanctuary found, love never dies.

Miracles Blossoming in Unity

In unity bright, our spirits bloom,
Creating miracles, dispelling gloom.
With every heart that joins the song,
Together we rise, we all belong.

In countless hands, we weave the thread,
Of love and hope, where angels tread.
With open hearts, our voices blend,
In harmony's grace, let joy transcend.

Through trials faced, we hold the light,
Guiding each other through darkest night.
A tapestry rich with colors bold,
In unity's warmth, our love unfolds.

Each miracle born from kindness shown,
In shared embrace, we are not alone.
For in the bond of spirit's grace,
Life's sweetest joys we can embrace.

Together we rise, together we stand,
In sacred circles, hand in hand.
In miracles blossoming, faith ignites,
A world transformed by love's true sights.

Divine Intertwining

In morning light, we seek Your face,
Hearts aflame with holy grace.
Threads of love, together spun,
In every soul, Your will be done.

As rivers flow to oceans wide,
In faith we walk, You are our guide.
With every prayer, our spirits rise,
In Your embrace, our fears subside.

In whispered winds, Your presence near,
A gentle touch dispels all fear.
With open arms, we draw You close,
In every breath, we love the most.

Our lives entwined, a sacred dance,
In shadows deep, we find romance.
Unity in every tear,
In joy and sorrow, You are here.

So let us praise in harmony,
For we are one, eternally.
As stars align in evening's glow,
We celebrate the love we know.

The Joyful Sacrament

In gathered hearts, we lift our voice,
Together in this holy choice.
With bread and wine, we find the light,
A sacred bond that shines so bright.

In laughter shared, in tears we flow,
Each moment blooms, a sacred glow.
With open arms, we welcome grace,
In every heart, a holy space.

The music swells, the spirit sings,
In unity, our soul takes wing.
Through every trial, hand in hand,
In love's embrace, we firmly stand.

As we behold the gift of life,
In peace, we conquer every strife.
Together in this hallowed place,
We weave a tapestry of grace.

So let us rise, in faith take flight,
With joyful hearts, we share the light.
In every soul, a spark divine,
Forever blessed, in love we shine.

Prayerful Affection

In whispered prayers, our hearts collide,
With tender love, You are our guide.
In every sigh, a sacred plea,
With open hearts, we come to Thee.

Through valleys low and mountains high,
In darkest night, You hear our cry.
Each joyful moment, every tear,
In prayerful silence, You are near.

With hands held tight, we face the storm,
In faith, we find Your loving form.
Through trials faced and lessons learned,
In every heart, Your flame has burned.

In gratitude, we lift our song,
For in Your arms, we all belong.
With humble hearts, we seek Your face,
In prayerful affection, we find grace.

In every breath, a thankfulness,
In quiet moments, we find rest.
Together bound, in love so profound,
In prayer, our solace will be found.

The Richness of Promise

In every dawn, we see Your light,
A tapestry of truth in sight.
Your promises, like stars above,
Guide us gently, wrapped in love.

In aching hearts, Your whispers soar,
With every beat, we long for more.
In trials faced, we hold on tight,
For in Your gaze, we find our might.

With faith as our enduring shield,
In every wound, Your love is healed.
With joy as deep as oceans wide,
In every soul, You will abide.

In freedom found, we rise and sing,
With hearts ablaze, we share the spring.
For every promise, pure and true,
In richest faith, we trust in You.

So let us walk, hand in hand we go,
Through valleys low and mountains slow.
In every shadow, we will see,
The richness of Your love in me.

Blessings in Every Glance

In every look a light shines bright,
Joy flows forth in sacred sight.
With hearts aligned, we lift our gaze,
Grateful souls in endless praise.

In laughter shared, in quiet prayer,
The love of God is ever there.
Through trials faced and burdens borne,
We rise anew with each sweet morn.

In whispered winds, His voice we hear,
A gentle touch that calms our fear.
Through every glance, His hand we find,
In sacred love, our souls entwined.

As moments pass, like fleeting dreams,
We find our hope in love's sweet beams.
In every glance, our blessings flow,
Together, Holy Spirit, we grow.

With each embrace, a prayer is sent,
A bond unbroken, pure ascent.
In every glance, we learn to see,
The endless blessings meant to be.

The Altar of Our Union

Upon the altar, hearts unite,
In faith and love, we share the light.
With vows that echo through the years,
We find our strength through joy and tears.

Together we stand, hand in hand,
A life of service, side by side.
In every challenge, love will guide,
On this great journey, we will stride.

Each moment cherished, sacred space,
In every trial, we find His grace.
Through laughter shared and trials faced,
In love's embrace, our fears displaced.

With hymns of praise, our voices rise,
Our spirits soar beyond the skies.
In unity, we find our song,
In every heart, where we belong.

The altar stands, a beacon bright,
Where love ignites, dispelling night.
In sacred union, we remain,
Forever blessed, through joy and pain.

Harmony in the Sacred Dance

In rhythm soft, our souls align,
A melody of love divine.
With every step, His grace we share,
In sacred dance, we find our prayer.

Through swirling grace, we move in time,
Our hearts united, pure and chime.
With gentle sway, our spirits lift,
In every moment, love's sweet gift.

The music flows, both wild and free,
In harmony, we find our plea.
With joyful hearts, we celebrate,
In sacred unity, we elevate.

Through trials faced, our strength will grow,
In every step, His love we know.
As sacred rhythms guide our way,
We dance together, night and day.

In sacred circles, hand in hand,
We weave a tapestry so grand.
With every twirl, we share his trance,
In every breath, the sacred dance.

Covenant of the Kindred

In bonds of love, a promise made,
Hearts intertwined, we're not afraid.
Through every storm and trial's test,
In sacred covenant, we find rest.

Together walking this holy path,
We share His joy, erasing wrath.
With open arms and hearts so true,
In every moment, we renew.

Our kinship deepens, love unfolds,
Through stories shared and hands to hold.
With whispers soft, we share our fears,
In faith and trust, we dry each other's tears.

With every word, our spirits blend,
A sacred truth that has no end.
In unity, we rise and stand,
A covenant blessed, forever planned.

Through trials faced, our hopes ignite,
In every soul, His love alight.
In every heartbeat, every sigh,
We sing our bond, the by and by.

The Sacred Covenant

In silence we gather, hearts intertwined,
With prayers like whispers, our souls aligned.
The sacred vow lingers, binding us close,
In faith we journey, together we chose.

Beneath the heavens, stars brightly gleam,
Our covenant glows, a divine dream.
Through trials and blessings, together we'll stand,
In love's gentle flame, forever we're planned.

The whispers of angels, our guides on this way,
In moments of doubt, they lead us to pray.
A promise unbroken, in grace we believe,
Together, forever, in love we shall cleave.

Each step on this journey, taken in trust,
With hearts full of hope, our spirits combust.
For in this connection, a miracle grows,
A sacred reminder of how true love flows.

In joy and in sorrow, our spirits renew,
The sacred covenant, eternally true.
With light as our beacon, forever we shine,
In the heart of the faithful, our spirits align.

Mending the Fractured Spirit

When shadows gather, and hope seems to flee,
Whispers of comfort remind us to see.
A touch of the sacred can heal every wound,
In silence, the spirit's sweet solace is found.

The heartache we carry, a burden we bear,
Yet faith is a bridge, connecting us there.
With trust as our anchor, we rise from the fall,
The spirit, once fractured, is whole after all.

In the warmth of compassion, we bathe in the light,
Each prayer a beacon, dispelling the night.
Together we gather, our voices a chant,
Mending the spirit, a beautiful grant.

Through trials, we blossom, like flowers in spring,
In the mourning of grief, new life we will bring.
The bonds that we form in the depths of our soul,
Are threads of connection that make us feel whole.

So let us remember, when days feel unkind,
The strength of our unity, love intertwined.
In mending our spirits, we find our way back,
In the fabric of kindness, we're never off track.

Love as Worship

In every soft gesture, our hearts come alive,
Each moment of kindness, where love can thrive.
The smile of a stranger, a warm, gentle touch,
In acts of pure love, we worship so much.

Through trials and triumphs, we offer our thanks,
In the depths of our hearts, where gratitude ranks.
For love is the essence, the prayer we can sing,
In the rhythm of kindness, our spirits take wing.

The warmth of compassion, like sunlight, it glows,
In the heart of the weary, its beauty bestows.
Every heartbeat is sacred, a note in the choir,
In loving each other, we rise ever higher.

With every kind word, we craft our own grace,
In union, we find the divine face to face.
To love is to worship, to cherish, to give,
In the dance of our lives, together we live.

So let every moment be filled with our song,
In love as our worship, forever belong.
In the journey of faith, may our hearts ever yearn,
To bask in the warmth of the love we discern.

The Divine Tapestry

Woven together, each thread is a soul,
In the loom of creation, we play a great role.
Each color a story, a truth we embrace,
In the divine tapestry, we find our grace.

With hands joined in prayer, our wishes take flight,
In the fabric of hope, we ignite the light.
Through laughter and sorrow, the weaver's own plan,
In the beauty of love, united we stand.

The patterns of life, a journey we'll weave,
Through seasons of sorrow, we learn to believe.
In the dark of the night, our colors will shine,
In the design of the cosmos, eternally twine.

Each thread a connection, each knot a new bond,
In the heart of the world, we find where we've conned.
Together we flourish, forever entwined,
In the divine tapestry, love shall remind.

So let us be patient, as frays may appear,
In the hands of the Master, we've nothing to fear.
The tapestry holds, through time and through space,
Our lives intertwined, an infinite grace.

Embracing the Sacred Frequency

In whispers soft, the spirit sings,
Awakening hearts to holy things.
A rhythm pure, the soul's delight,
In sacred vibrations, we find our light.

The call of grace, it beckons near,
A chorus bright, dispelling fear.
In every heartbeat, a chance to dance,
To join the tune of divine romance.

Through trials faced, the echoes swell,
In unity, our stories tell.
Embracing each note, a symphony,
We weave our lives in harmony.

From mountains high to valleys deep,
In prayerful silence, we dare to leap.
With faith as our anchor, we rise above,
In every breath, we find His love.

In sacred spaces, we take our place,
A gathering of souls in grace.
With open hearts, we seek to find,
The sacred frequency that binds mankind.

The Light of Forgiveness

In shadows cast, the heart retreats,
Yet in forgiveness, love repeats.
A gentle touch to heal the pain,
In letting go, we break the chain.

The whisper soft, a guiding flare,
Illuminates the dark despair.
With open arms, we find our way,
In every dawn, a brand new day.

Each step we take, a chance to mend,
In mercy's glow, we learn to bend.
For every fracture, a chance to heal,
In love's embrace, our hearts reveal.

The burdens lifted with a sigh,
In sacred moments, we learn to fly.
A tapestry of grace and trust,
In every heartbeat, we rise from dust.

Through trials faced, the spirit grows,
In the light of forgiveness, beauty flows.
Let us extend our hands in prayer,
For in forgiving, love is rare.

Divine Love's Footprints

In every step, a path is shown,
With footprints marked, we are not alone.
A walk of faith, where spirits soar,
In divine love, we are restored.

The journey wide, the road unfolds,
With guidance pure, our story molds.
Across the sands of time and grace,
We find our home in His embrace.

Through valleys dark and mountains high,
Each tear we shed becomes a sigh.
A dance in grace, we rise anew,
In every crack, His light breaks through.

With every heartbeat, love's refrain,
A melody that soothes the pain.
In whispered prayers, we lift our voice,
For in His love, we rejoice.

As seasons change, the footprints fade,
Yet in our hearts, His love is laid.
With every step, a sacred trust,
In divine love, we live, we must.

Serene Pilgrimage

With humble hearts, we start the quest,
On paths of peace, we find our rest.
Each journey taken, a sacred song,
In harmony, we all belong.

Through trials faced, our spirits rise,
In faith we walk beneath the skies.
In nature's grace, we find the way,
With every dawn, a brand new day.

The winding road, a sacred dance,
In moments still, we seize the chance.
With every step, we seek the light,
In prayerful whispers throughout the night.

The sacred soil beneath our feet,
In quietude, our souls repeat.
With open eyes, the truth appears,
In every blessing, we shed our fears.

As pilgrims strong, we journey forth,
In shared belief, we find our worth.
With hearts ablaze, we walk in grace,
In serene pilgrimage, we find His face.

Celestial Union

In the heavens, a light so divine,
Hearts entwined in a love that feels right.
Angels whisper of a bond so rare,
Guiding us gently, boundless care.

Across the stars, we sing our praise,
In this embrace, our spirits blaze.
Faith leads us on through trials and night,
Together we rise, reaching new height.

With every heartbeat, our prayers ascend,
In the stillness, His grace we commend.
Eternity calls, as we walk in grace,
Hand in hand, in this holy space.

Beneath the moon's shimmering glow,
In sacred moments, true love will show.
Soulmates united, forever we stand,
In the cosmos, together we've planned.

With hearts ablaze, we turn to the light,
In this celestial dance, pure and bright.
For love is our bond, through storm and strife,
A union in faith, eternal life.

Wings of Devotion

On wings of faith, our spirits soar high,
In the presence of love, we draw nigh.
Each gentle whisper, a promise we keep,
In the arms of devotion, our souls leap.

Through trials faced, and shadows we tread,
With trust in our hearts, no fear, no dread.
With every prayer, our spirits entwine,
In the garden of hope, our light will shine.

In sacred realms, where angels abide,
With wings of devotion, we take our stride.
The path is clear, illuminated by grace,
In this dance of love, we find our place.

So let us spread our wings and take flight,
In the embrace of love, darkness turns bright.
Together we journey, hearts intertwined,
In the haven of faith, peace we will find.

With every heartbeat, our vows we renew,
Wings of devotion, steadfast and true.
In the chorus of life, our voices will blend,
A melody sweet, that will never end.

Redemption of the Soul

In valleys low, where shadows reside,
Hope whispers softly, a guiding tide.
Through trials of heart, we seek the light,
Redemption blooms, breaking the night.

From ashes of sorrow, we rise anew,
With faith as our anchor, steadfast and true.
The soul's journey, a path to embrace,
In the arms of mercy, we find our grace.

Each tear that falls, a river of peace,
In moments of stillness, our worries cease.
For in every struggle, strength will unfold,
A story of courage, divine and bold.

With hands lifted high, we reach for the sky,
In joyful surrender, we learn to fly.
The dawn brings promise of brighter days,
In the arms of redemption, our spirits blaze.

So let the past fade, like mist in the morn,
In a garden of love, our hearts reborn.
Embracing the light, we dance to the song,
Of redemption and grace, where we all belong.

The Garden of Tenderness

In the garden of tenderness, blooms of love,
Where hearts find solace, guided from above.
With each gentle breeze, a caress divine,
In the silence of evening, our spirits align.

Among the petals, soft whispers we share,
In the light of the moon, we lay our cares bare.
The fragrance of hope lingers in the air,
In this sacred space, our worries we wear.

As sunlight breaks through, casting warmth on the ground,

In the garden of love, true joy is found.
We nurture each other, like blossoms in bloom,
In the embrace of tenderness, we banish the gloom.

With roots intertwined, we stand ever near,
In this holy refuge, we conquer our fear.
Love's gentle whispers will guide us each day,
In the garden of the heart, we find our way.

So let us plant seeds of compassion and grace,
As we wander together through this sacred space.
For in the garden of tenderness, we grow,
In the warmth of His love, our spirits will flow.

Anointed Paths of Togetherness

In the light we gather, side by side,
With faith as our compass, hearts open wide.
Together we walk, through shadows and sun,
Anointed by love, our journey begun.

United in purpose, hand in hand we stand,
Each step is a blessing, guided by His hand.
Through trials and triumphs, we find our way,
Anointed paths lead us, come what may.

With prayers as our anchor, we rise above,
Together we flourish, in grace and in love.
Embracing the whispers of hope in the night,
Anointed by grace, we shine ever bright.

The echoes of laughter, a sweet symphony,
In harmony's dance, our lives intertwined.
Each heartbeats a promise, a sacred decree,
Anointed paths show us how love's designed.

So let us be vessels, of kindness and peace,
In the garden of friendship, let blessings increase.
Together we flourish, forever we'll strive,
On anointed paths, together we thrive.

The Gospel of Togetherness

In stories of old, we find our refrain,
The gospel of love, shared over again.
With hearts that are open, we gather as one,
In the warmth of togetherness, battles are won.

With hands stretched in kindness, we greet every soul,
The gospel of togetherness, makes broken hearts whole.
In prayerful communion, our spirits align,
Together we journey, in grace we entwine.

Through valleys of sorrow, the peaks of delight,
The gospel of caring shines endlessly bright.
With voices united, we sing out our plea,
In the gospel of togetherness, all are set free.

Embracing each moment, with laughter and tears,
The gospel reminds us, we conquer our fears.
In the circle of trust, we share and we grow,
The gospel of togetherness, carries that glow.

So let us be messengers, of peace and of light,
In the gospel of love, we stand firm and right.
Together we journey, our hearts interlace,
In the gospel of togetherness, we find our true place.

Revelations of the Heart's Journey

In quiet reflection, our hearts gently sigh,
Revelations unfold, as the moments pass by.
Each tear tells a story, each smile holds a prayer,
In the depths of our being, His love is laid bare.

Through valleys of struggle, the mountains of grace,
We seek in the darkness, each shimmering trace.
Revelations awaken, illuminate the way,
In the heart's sacred journey, love will never sway.

With each gentle whisper, we find our own truth,
Revelations of wisdom, bestowed in our youth.
The light that we carry, shines bright from within,
In the revelations of love, each day we begin.

Bound by the promise, the journey is clear,
Revelations of courage, dispelling all fear.
In the rhythm of life, our spirits will rise,
Together we witness, God's love in our eyes.

So let us embrace, all the lessons we learn,
Revelations of the heart, in our spirits they burn.
In the tapestry woven, let love be our guide,
Through revelations of faith, we walk side by side.

A Covenant of Fresh Beginnings

In the dawn of each morning, a promise unfolds,
A covenant of fresh starts, as each heart consoles.
With open embraces, we welcome the day,
In the warmth of our union, our fears melt away.

Through challenges faced, we rise from the dust,
A covenant of hope, in togetherness trust.
With intentions of kindness, we weave our own fate,
In this new beginning, love conquers all hate.

With prayers as our fabric, we stitch every seam,
A covenant of joy, in each shared dream.
In the bloom of togetherness, we find our true worth,
A covenant of blessings, rejoicing our birth.

So let us remember, the vows that we take,
A covenant of love, no matter the stake.
With grace as our anchor, we'll weather the storm,
In a covenant of unity, our spirits keep warm.

With faith as our guide, and courage our strength,
A covenant of beginnings stretches wide its length.
Together we flourish, in trust we abide,
In this sacred journey, let love be our guide.

The Alchemy of Affection

In the garden of hearts, love blooms bright,
Transforming the mundane into pure light.
Each glance a potion, each touch a grace,
In the alchemy of affection, we find our place.

Through trials and tears, our spirits entwine,
In the crucible of trust, destinies align.
With gentle whispers, the soul gives birth,
To a new dawn rising, a rebirth of worth.

Hand in hand, we journey through pain,
Together we weather the fiercest rain.
The essence of kindness, a sacred art,
In the alchemy of affection, love binds the heart.

From candlelit moments to laughter shared,
In the tapestry of life, we are carefully paired.
With each shared dream, new paths we create,
In the dance of affection, our fate does await.

Together we rise, through shadows we weave,
In the symphony of souls, we dare to believe.
In the heart's true treasure, we seek and defend,
For in love's true alchemy, we find the end.

Sacred Whispers Between Souls

In silent corners where shadows meld,
Reside the whispers that the heart has held.
Each sigh and laughter, a sacred thread,
Binding our stories, where love has led.

Beneath the starlit skies, we roam free,
Each heartbeat a chapter in time's decree.
With gentle grace, our spirits connect,
In sacred whispers, we earn respect.

With every prayer, a promise unfolds,
In the warmth of friendship, a treasure holds.
The light in your eyes, a beacon so bright,
Guiding me home through the darkest night.

Together we wander down paths unknown,
In the quiet moments, love has grown.
Our souls make music, a celestial song,
In sacred whispers, we truly belong.

In the tapestry of life, our threads entwine,
Each stitch a memory, a design divine.
Embraced by the silence, our hearts take flight,
In sacred whispers, we dance in the light.

Regeneration of the Spirit

In the stillness of the night, hope is born,
From the ashes of doubt, the spirit is worn.
Through trials of faith, we find our way,
In the regeneration of spirit, we choose to stay.

With open arms, we welcome the dawn,
In the embrace of love, our fears are drawn.
Through storms of sorrow, we rise and heal,
In the regeneration of spirit, our truth is sealed.

Each tear that falls is a seed of grace,
Cultivating courage, it creates space.
For with every heartbeat, we learn to mend,
In the circle of life, where beginnings blend.

In kindness shown, the spirit ignites,
Shattering darkness, revealing the lights.
In the warmth of community, our essence grows,
In the regeneration of spirit, love overflows.

So let us wander, hand in hand in faith,
In the garden of life, we discover our wraith.
Forever reborn, in joy we bask,
In the regeneration of spirit, love is our task.

Grace Unfolding in Each Moment

In quiet reflections, grace takes its flight,
Through every heartbeat, a dance in the light.
In simple pleasures, we find the divine,
Grace unfolding gently, in spaces benign.

Through laughter shared and hands held tight,
Grace weaves its magic in the softest light.
In trials we face, it teaches us bold,
In the canvas of life, true stories unfold.

With every sunrise, a blessing bestowed,
In the heartbeat of nature, we lighten the load.
As shadows fade, we embrace the day,
In grace unfolding, love finds its way.

Moments of kindness, a whisper, a smile,
In the weave of our journeys, we pause for a while.
In gratitude's chorus, our hearts align,
In grace unfolding, our spirits intertwine.

So cherish each moment, let love define,
In grace unfolding, our lives intertwine.
For in each breath, a miracle lies,
In grace and connection, our spirit flies.

The Epiphany of Us

In silence we seek Your guiding light,
Awakening souls in the depths of night.
With hearts open wide, Your presence we face,
Together we find our sacred space.

Through trials and storms, our faith shall stand,
A tapestry woven by Your gentle hand.
In every whisper, Your love we discern,
A flame of devotion, forever to burn.

With eyes set on truth, we walk the path,
In the warmth of Your love, we conquer wrath.
As we gather in prayer, hearts beat as one,
In the embrace of the Spirit, our journey begun.

We rise with the dawn, His mercy our song,
In unity thriving, where we all belong.
In the stillness of grace, we find our way,
Together in faith, we shall not stray.

Our hearts intertwined in divine embrace,
In the epiphany of us, we find our place.
For every moment, a gift from above,
In the dance of our spirits, we flourish in love.

Cherished by the Almighty

In the cradle of grace, we find our worth,
Each moment a blessing upon this earth.
With hands lifted high, we sing and rejoice,
Cherished by the Almighty, we find our voice.

Through valleys and peaks, His mercy shall flow,
In the depths of our hearts, His presence we know.
With every tear shed, He wipes them away,
In the love of the Father, we find our stay.

Together we gather beneath heavenly skies,
In union we thrive, with hope in our eyes.
Cherished with kindness, His light ever near,
In the warmth of compassion, we have no fear.

In laughter and sorrow, His promises claim,
In the richness of love, we honor His name.
Finding strength in each other, we rise above,
Cherished by the Almighty, we flourish in love.

In the cadence of faith, we walk hand in hand,
Together we'll traverse this sacred land.
From the depths of our spirits, His truth we proclaim,
In the heart of the faithful, we find peace in His name.

Journey of Grace

On a path woven by fate's gentle hand,
We travel together, across this vast land.
With hope in our hearts and faith as our guide,
In the journey of grace, we shall abide.

Through shadows that linger and doubts that arise,
We seek the light hidden behind cloudy skies.
In whispers of love, His promises flow,
In the journey of grace, we learn to let go.

With each step we take, His presence will grow,
In our hearts lies a truth only He can bestow.
With courage ignited, our spirits will soar,
In the journey of grace, we discover much more.

Encircled by beauty, we dance in His care,
In the silence of prayer, we feel Him so near.
With hearts intertwined, we draw ever close,
In the journey of grace, His love we can boast.

Together we rise, as the dawn breaks anew,
In the warmth of His light, our spirits grew.
For every moment shared, a treasure embraced,
In the journey of grace, we forever find grace.

Revelations of the Heart

In the stillness of night, a whisper so sweet,
The revelations of the heart, profound and complete.
With love as our armor, the truth shall unfold,
In the light of His wisdom, we cherish the bold.

Each heartbeat a message, each breath a prayer,
In the sacred connection, we find solace rare.
With eyes wide open, we search for the spark,
In the revelations of the heart, we venture from dark.

Through the trials of life, we gather the threads,
In the fabric of faith, where hope gently spreads.
With hearts intertwined, we illuminate the way,
In the revelations of the heart, love shall stay.

In the tapestry woven, by grace we are bound,
In His profound mercy, true peace can be found.
With each gentle whisper, the Spirit will start,
In the revelations of the heart, grace plays its part.

So let us rejoice in this journey we share,
With faith as our compass, we flourish in prayer.
In the revelations of the heart, we sing our song,
In the embrace of divine love, we eternally belong.

Messages from the Dawn of Togetherness

In the soft light of morn, we stand,
In unity, hand in hand.
Voices rise in a sacred song,
Together, we shall right the wrong.

The sun greets our hopeful eyes,
In every heart, a shared surprise.
As gentle breezes whisper low,
The seeds of love begin to grow.

Each moment gifted, a prayer's breath,
In harmony, we conquer death.
Together we tread the path of grace,
In each smile, the holy trace.

With kindred spirits, we are blessed,
In challenges, we find our rest.
For in this journey, side by side,
Together, we shall abide.

In the stillness, our souls entwine,
Witnessing the sacred design.
In every dawn, a promise pure,
In faith, our hearts shall endure.

Garden of Grace and Desire

In the garden where love does bloom,
Whispers of hope erase all gloom.
Petals dancing to the skies,
A reflection of divine replies.

Each fragrance tells a story sweet,
In this place, our spirits meet.
Underneath the bright blue dome,
Here in grace, we find our home.

With every heartbeat, a soft prayer,
In this sacred space, we share.
A tapestry of dreams entwined,
In each gaze, a love defined.

As seasons shift with gentle grace,
In every leaf, God's warm embrace.
We cultivate the soil of souls,
Where passion thrives and love consoles.

In this haven of tender light,
Every shadow melts from sight.
Together, we tend to our desires,
In the garden of holy fires.

The Beatitudes of Newfound Passion

Blessed are the hearts that find,
In love's warmth, a welcome kind.
With every touch, the soul ignites,
In passionate dance, our spirits take flight.

Blessed are those who dare to seek,
In gentle truths, the strong and meek.
With whispered dreams, we intertwine,
In newfound passion, our lives align.

Blessed are the tears that cleanse,
In vulnerability, love transcends.
Through trials faced, our bonds grow tight,
In the darkest hours, we find the light.

Blessed are the moments shared,
In the echo of voices paired.
For in this union, sacred and bold,
We uncover the stories untold.

Blessed are we, who choose to fight,
For love's greatest battles, day and night.
With gratitude for each breath shared,
In passion's embrace, forever prepared.

Rhapsody of the Beloved

In the rhapsody of our souls, we sing,
Each note a promise, love's offering.
With every heartbeat, the world's refrain,
In harmony, we dance through joy and pain.

In twilight's glow, your light does shine,
A tapestry woven with threads divine.
With every whisper, a secret told,
In your embrace, my heart unfolds.

As we wander through starry nights,
In the moon's embrace, our love ignites.
Each shared moment a sacred gift,
In the rhapsody, our spirits lift.

In the beauty of silence, we find our way,
Through shared dreams in night and day.
In the depths of love's sweet lore,
We discover what we're longing for.

Together, we craft this timeless song,
In laughter's echo, where we belong.
With every refrain, a sweet release,
In the rhapsody, our souls find peace.

Milton Keynes UK
Ingram Content Group UK Ltd.
UKHW020041271124
451585UK00012B/991